WINDOWS 8 SUCKS, BUT HERE'S HOW TO USE IT

KEN BARKER

DEDICATION

I dedicate this book to all the Windows 8 users who had to put up with it and look for books like this.

Thank YOU for purchasing this book. Look for other books in the series especially the Windows 9 book in 2015 – even though I don't think it is going to suck.

CONTENTS

ACKNOWLEDGMENTS

Thanks to anyone who encouraged me on my writing.
Thank you Kristyn Fyffe for your help with editing.
Research done at Microsoft.com, Winsupersite.com,
Lifehacker.com, Wikipedia.org
Referenced classicShell.net, Stardock.com for 3rd party programs.
Screen captures by Windows Sniping tool and Techsmith's Snagit
available at www.techsmith.com.
All images in this book are screen captures or photos taken by the
author.

PREFACE

Let me start off by saying "I love Windows." I use Windows – I even installed 8 on my MacBook Air (which I have because it is one of the best laptops to run Windows on, and I need to be familiar with Mac's for work).
I am not a Windows hater who just puts down anything Microsoft does. I Promoted Windows Vista **and** ME (Millennium) when they came out and everyone complained about them as we are about 8. "If you take some time to learn how to use it, you will be fine" I said. "Things change and you just have to go with it" I would explain. I liked the look, I liked the new features, I even liked how "Control Panel" and other functions Where re organized.

Windows Vista and ME also had many complaints about system crashes, software compatibility, and other usage issues not related to the user interface. Windows 8 is **not** having these issues.

I believe the main problem with Windows Visa and ME where that so many people bought cheap computers or upgraded older computers with not enough RAM memory or processor power. So the computes that people where using just where not able to run the new OS. I blame Microsoft and computer manufacturers for promoting both the upgrade and cheap computers as being able to run these OS's.

When Windows 8 was first released to enthusiasts and then the public a few months later, I liked it just like I did Vista. It was after I used the final version for a few months that I had to go back to using Windows 7. I could not copy and paste info from the mail app, it was impossible to get the charms bar when you wanted it (still is), and it is impossible to find the app or program you want from the default windows Start screen. Being a computer technician, I also find it very difficult to do repairs on systems with 8. Microsoft and the manufactures introduced some security features (sounds like a good idea), but people are still getting virus' and it's a pain for us to do diagnostics and repairs.

In my opinion the Windows 8 user interface just sucks!

It is just designed for a tablet or touch interface, not a normal keyboard and mouse computer.

But since so many people **need to use it**, I'm going to tell you **how to use it** - for the general computer user.

Read on ye traveler.

1 How to use this book

This book is designed to cover the basic operation of Windows 8.1 (8), not every feature of Windows. It addresses the user interface mostly, not settings or program features. It may not explain every step, so you may need to follow the on screen prompts at times. I only do this when it is obvious at that point and there could be different options to choose depending on the goal.

This book will focus on mouse and keyboard users of windows 8. Touch will be referenced but not explained in detail. Many people don't even use touch if they have it, much less the target audience of this book.

I will specify differences in 8 and 8.1, but will refer to the overall operating system and experience as Windows 8 or just 8.

Following menu prompts.

Directions on how to click through a series of menus or options will use the **>** symbol to mean "Then click on" and look like this.

For example: *To get to the Power button to turn off your computer: Open Charms > Settings > Power.*

What to call the Start screen interface?

When Windows 8 was in pre-release "Beta" testing, the new Tile interface was called "Metro". Microsoft Changed the name to "Modern" after German retailer Metro AG sued over the use of the Metro name. Most people who ever heard Metro, still call it that. It is also referred to as the Tile interface because of the multi squares and rectangles used.

I will usually refer to it as the Tile interface in this book, I think it is easier to remember because people understand what a Tile is.

The Book

I am basing what is covered in this book on my experience with talking to customers and my personal frustrations of the past 3 years. I will be stating my opinion about many features as I explain them or how to use them.

There might even been some humor or at least some non-serious statements.

The book is published in a 6x8 format so it is not too big to be kept near or on your computer desk!

Moving on

Flip the pages to the left to move to the next page, read those pages, and repeat. ☺

2 FIRST THINGS FIRST

Do Windows updates then the 8.1 update ASAP.

As with any new computer, make sure you do all the Windows Updates you can. If you encounter errors doing all 110+ all at once, you can do 20 or so at a time. If you can be patient, Windows will install updates as you go over the first few days. If you have had the computer for a while before getting this book, then you may only have a few to do.

The 8.1 update makes the computer much easier to use and this book is written with it in mind - with 8.0 differences noted.

Many people ran into issues running the 8.1 update before doing all of the other Windows updates first. So to avoid those problems I will suggest checking for updates a couple times even when you are told there are no updates. Windows 8 seems to pick some updates up after sitting for a while.

How to Use It...

Doing Windows Updates:

From the Desktop > Right-click the Start button > Control Panel > System and Security > under the Windows Update section click on "Check for updates".

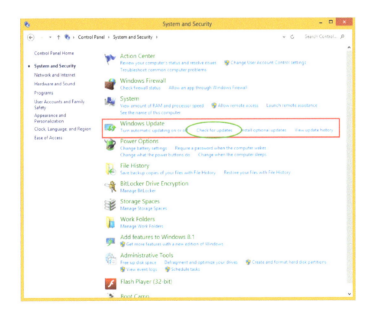

From here you can follow the prompts just as you did for windows 7 or earlier when it shows you the list of updates available.

If you do 20 or so at a time, start from the bottom of the list since they are usually in reverse order of when they were released. Check as many boxes as you can see on the page without scrolling, then click on "Install updates".

You may have to restart the computer after each group is done. Then repeat the process until all the updates are done.

Get ready for the 8.1 Update:

*Backup any pictures, documents, or anything you can't loose. Always backup before a major update. Even though it's highly unlikely you will lose anything…… Better to be safe than sorry.

This is a long process. Like 2-4 hours long! You can use the computer while it is downloading and processing.
When it is done with the update, you will need to go through the same setup process as when you first got the computer and choose a User Name and everything….

It could take a couple of hours to download, and you can keep using the computer until it finishes. It will also take an hour or so to do the actual update.

Like I said, it is a long process

I suggest starting the process before going to bed or work, and be ready to finish when you get back to the computer.

Doing the 8.1 Update:

To do the 8.1 update, you need to go to the new App Store located in the Tile or Start screen. Click on the Store Tile. You should see the 8.1 update as the largest program as soon as the Store loads. Click on that Tile / App and follow the prompts.

When it is done with the update, you will need to go through the same setup process as when you first got the computer and choose a User Name and everything…. Your data and programs will still be unless there was some major error or you chose to create a different user name at this point.

3 THE USER NAME

DO NOT use your email address as your User Name for Windows 8!

Another mistake I think Microsoft made was in the User Name section of the setup of Windows 8.
In an attempt to make everything you do linked together and synced online, Microsoft has you use your Hotmail, Outlook.com, Xbox, or any other Microsoft account as your user name.

They make it look like you have no choice, but you do. It is just hidden deep in a couple links. You **can** link you Microsoft account later.

There are several problems that come up because of using your email as a User name, some of which I bet Microsoft did not even consider.

The first problem is that many people were confused by this option. In the past all you did was put in a name and maybe a password. Now it looks like you have to have a Hotmail (Microsoft) account. Although most people do have one already, many people don't remember it or know they have one!

So this brings in the frustration of **having** to create a new Microsoft email account for many people who just want to click "next" and get their computer up and running.

The second problem (The one I bet Microsoft did not think about.) that comes up is if people forget their email password or there is some other issue with logging into the Microsoft accounts, the person is locked out of their computer.
Of course the password is there to protect your computer, but having it linked to an email address makes it much harder to solve the "I forgot my password" problem. This happens more than you may think.

Since This Microsoft account is often made is haste, people often don't remember what other email they used as a backup or their cell phone number has changed – which can also be used to reset your password.
So I or other technicians have to try and bypass the password, or backup the person's data, erase everything, and reinstall windows – just because the User Name is linked to an email address.

The third issue (I also doubt MS thought about.) I have with this system is that when someone takes their computer to a technician, like me, or anyone else – a friend or coworker who says they are good with computers (Don't always believe these people. "good with" and being able to work on a computer are 2 different things.) - you need to give that person or company your email password to work on the computer!

This is a major security flaw.

 I would hope you can trust whomever you choose to work on your computer, but email passwords can give people access to very sensitive information. In today's world, you should not trust anyone with this info if you can help it.

Visit my computer and technology news site *TechBreakdown.tv* and search for "passwords" for information and articles on passwords and security.

How to get around the email address:

First time setup:
On the **Sign in to your PC screen**, *where it asks for your email address, move down to the bottom of the screen and find:*

"Sign in without a Microsoft account?" link on the lower left of the screen and click it. > *"Local account" button on the lower right of the next screen.*

This will allow you to create a normal User Name or Local Account.

8.1 update :

*On the **Sign in to your Microsoft Account** screen, where it asks for your email address, move down to the bottom of the screen and find:*

*"**Create a new Account**" link on the lower left of the screen and click it. > "**Continue using my existing Account**" link on the bottom left of the next page.*

Remove or disconnect your email from your user name:

If you already used your Microsoft email to log into 8, you can disconnect it anytime. If you have not done the 8.1 update yet, I would disconnect it before doing the update.

Start from the Tile or Start screen > Type "account settings" > "Your account settings"(8.0 users may need to click on "Settings" first) in the search pane that opens. > "Disconnect" near the top of the screen under your User Name and email address. > enter password when prompted. > Enter new user name and password (if desired). > "Next" > "Sign out and Finish"

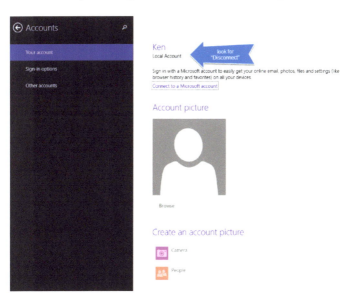

The computer may think for a few minutes, but it will return you to your Tile screen shortly.

*Microsoft Account Prompts -

You may be prompted to **Switch to a Microsoft Account** for various apps like People and Store.
* **_Do Not_** just ender your password when they tell you to "Switch to a Microsoft account", instead use the "Sign into each app separately instead (not recommended)" link at the bottom of the window that opens.

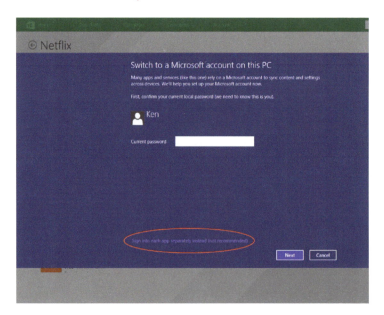

P.S. The new Microsoft Office (Word, Excel..) does make you use an Microsoft account to install them onto your computers. Again, this causes a lot of frustration for many people trying to sign up or remember your account information. I suggest finding a copy of Office 2010 from **my** *TechBreakdown.tv > Store* or my *Windows-8-Sucks.com > Store*. (Both powered by Amazon.com) or other online retailers if you can.

4 THE START SCREEN

The screen Windows 8 defaults to is the new "Tile" interface with the many large boxes called Tiles. What most people do not understand is that this IS THE START MENU for Windows 8. This screen lists all the programs on the computer just like the Start Button does when you click it. It looks very nice with its "live" tiles where you can see online programs get updated right there without opening the full program.

The problem is Microsoft did not explain this Start Menu screen to the public well, and although you can move the tiles around and sort the list, it is not very easy to visually search this screen. It shows so much stuff that you cannot find what you want.

How to Use it...

- Move your most common programs to the first screen.
If you do a normal left click and hold the button down, you will be able to move the Tile to where ever you want.

- Remove the tiles you do not want to see.
This will not uninstall the program; just remove it from this screen. – Right click on the tile and chose "Delete".

- Use search to find a program. Another thing Microsoft did not explain well (even though it is there preferred method); is you can use search to quickly find a program.
If you simply start typing while on the Start Screen, you will be shown a list of matching programs. Try it by typing N then O then T and E. Before you finish typing Notepad, you will see it on or near the top of the list on your screen and you can just hit Enter if it is highlighted or click on it to open the program. Pressing the ESC key will erase what you have typed and you can start over.

This method of finding programs has been around since Vista, and I use it often. With Vista and 7, You click on the "Start Button", or hit the windows key on your keyboard and just start typing.

- **See All Programs.** 8.1 added a down arrow in a circle on the lower left of the Start Screen that will show you a list of programs with smaller icons in alphabetical order. Again, this is similar to using the old Start Button and clicking on "All Programs".

But even this is not right, because it does not show you all the programs…. It shows a selected list first, and then you have to move the screen over to start seeing a larger selection…… What???

- **Make a tile App a Desktop icon**. (Hold on tight, it's complicated) —*You can Right click the program Tile and choose "Open file location". This will open an Explorer window on the Desktop showing the file highlighted. Then you can right click the file name and choose "Send to" > "Desktop (create shortcut)".*

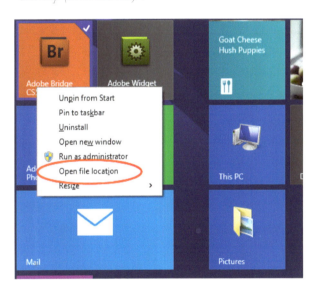

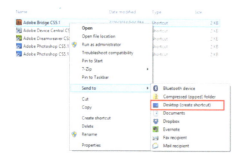

You can send a Tile to the Taskbar "Pin to Taskbar" by Right-clicking, but you can't move that icon to the Desktop, and if you do this for as many programs as you want, it will just fill up that taskbar and make it unusable.

- **Taskbar on the Tile screen.** The Taskbar will show itself on the Tile screen if you move your cursor to the very bottom of the screen below the slider bar. Sometimes you have to move it up and down a little for it to pop up. Then you can access your pinned programs or Right-click the Start button to get easy access to other settings. Yay!

-**How to move Tiles screens.** Theoretically you can move your mouse to the side of the screen, and if there are more programs in the list the tiles will move. This does not always seem to work for me; I always have to grab the window slider, or click the arrows at the bottom to move the Tiles.

You can also use 2 fingers to swipe left and right.

- **Name your Tile Groups**. You will notice that the tiles are separated in to groups of about 4 or 5 columns. If you move the Tiles around, you can group them however you want, then give a name to that group to make it easier to remember how you organized the Tiles.

To name a group, you need to click on the "-" at the lower right of the screen. This will show you all the Tiles in a zoomed out view called "semantic zoom". Now you can select a group and choose Name group from the app bar that appears at the top of the screen.

Yeah, I know pretty much no one will do this, but it's there if you want it

5 CHARMS

I would bet 98% of people see this chapter and think "Charms, What are those?"

Charms explained from Microsoft.com "The five charms—Search, Share, Start, Devices, and Settings—are quick ways to get to actions you do often, like search the web and your PC, print documents, and email photos and links. They're always available on the right side of your screen, no matter where you are in Windows"

As Microsoft explains, the Charms (A bar the appears on the right side of the screen) is supposed to be an easy way to access common functions. Unfortunately, most people just see this side bar menu as an annoying thing that pops up on them when they are trying to do something else and wont pop up when they need it. I am one of those people. I like the idea myself. But that bar is just so uncontrollable.
Most people do learn to use it to turn the computer off, but that is about it.

Charms gives you access to Searching the computer and internet, Sharing to social media or email, Devices like printers, and PC Settings.

How to Use it...

The Charms bar is a menu that slides in from the right side of the screen when you move your mouse to the right side corners of the screen. (Or swipe in from the right side if you are using touch).

Search is covered in Chapter 6

The Share and Devices Charms will only work when you are in an app / program. They do not work from the Desktop or Start screen except to tell you to open an app or to start an email.

Since social networks are taking over, it makes sense to make it easy to share items. Microsoft has to keep up.

If you are not a big sharer, I doubt you will use the Share feature much. On the other hand, since you know about it now, maybe you will…

- **Share**. *Open Charms > Share > Person or app > follow on screen prompts.*

This will let you send whatever you are doing to social media that you have linked to your account, or send the file to email or OneDrive. Other options can be available. *Not available in all apps, Works best with Microsoft Windows 8 apps. – Go figure…

- **Devices**. *Open Charms > Devices > Choose device.*

Here you can Print, send your screen to another monitor, or play a media file. Other options can be available. *Not available in all apps, Also works best with Microsoft Windows 8 apps.

- **Settings**. *Open Charms > Settings > Choose your setting.*

* Options differ if this is opened from the Desktop or Modern interface.

  If opened from a Microsoft app, you will get settings for that specific program.

Here you can see and access various PC settings. Directly accessible settings at the bottom of the menu are Internet connection, Volume, Brightness, and Power. (These are covered in Chapter 7, except Brightness; which I hope is obvious.)

There is also a **Change PC Settings** at the bottom that will take you to the Windows 8 "Control Panel" where you can change various Microsoft and Windows 8 features, but is not as powerful or easy to use as the traditional Control Panel.

From the Desktop you have access to Personalization, PC info, and Control Panel.

- **Personalization**. Here you can change your Background, Screen saver and other visual options.

- **PC Info**. Here you can see basic information about your computer like processor speed and amount of ram.

- **Control Panel**. Here you can access all of the computer settings. This is the traditional Control Panel found in Windows versions since the beginning. This is the screen I use to access the computer settings while working on customer computers because it has more features and is easier to use.

From the Modern interface you have access to Personalize, Tiles, and Help

- **Personalize**. Here you can change your system background colors and themes.

- **Tiles**. Here you can choose to see more programs in the Tile view including Administrative tools (Control Panel).

- **Help**. Here you can access Microsoft.com's Help about the Start screen.

6 SHUTDOWN, SEARCH, USER
WIRELESS, AND VOLUME

Turning off the computer has been an issue for many people ever since the "Start" button was introduced in Windows 95. For 20 years, you have needed to click the "Start" button (then choose "Shutdown") to turn the computer off. I talk to many people who still don't know this and just press the physical power button they use to turn the computer on. This feature has also been the source for many Windows related jokes.

Well, believe it or not, Windows 8 made it even harder. You needed to open the new "Charms" bar on the right side of the screen then go to Settings. Who would find that on their own?

8.1 added a quick link to Power at the top right of the Tiles Start screen. 8.1 also added a quick link to Search.

How to Use it...

The "Charms" bar was covered in more detail in chapter 7, I will just introduce it here in order to access the features we need to talk about now.

The Charms bar is a menu that slides in from the right side of the screen when you move your mouse to the right side corners of the Start screen. (Or swipe in from the right side if you are using touch). Among other features, it gives access to the "Shutdown" and "search" buttons, as well as wireless, and volume controls.

- **Turn off the computer or Shutdown**.
Open Charms > Settings > Power. Once you click on Power, you can choose from a Shutdown (Turn off), Sleep, Hibernate, or Restart. (All options may not be available depending on your computer)

8.1 added a second Power button to the top right of the screen next to the User name and image. This made it much easier, because sooooo many people did not know to look in the charms > Settings, and because the Charms menu is so hard to bring up.

- **Search**. There are several ways to search now with 8.1.
Click on the Search icon in the top right corner of the screen. **Or** *Right-click the Start Button* > *Search.* **Or** *from the Desktop* > *Open Charms* > *Search.* The last option is your only choice in 8.0 Desktop.

From the Tiles screen you can also simply start typing. Search results will appear on the screen.

You can search for programs, files, or the internet from this one location. By default, it will search "Everywhere". So if you are just looking for a file, you can click on the dropdown above the Search box and choose "files". Otherwise you may get too many results to be helpful. Windows tries to sort the results in to names of programs, files and probable web sites on top.

8.1 added a second Search button to the top right of the screen next to the new Power button.

- **User Name**. If you click on your user name in the upper right corner, you can choose to lock the computer, sign out, switch user, or change account picture.

- **Wireless / Internet**.
Open Charms > *Settings* > *Wireless icon.* Or Right-click Start Button > This is where you can see your wireless or internet connection options. You can also see your internet connection information from the wireless icon in the right side of the Taskbar on the desktop.

- **Volume**.

Open Charms > Settings > Volume icon.

This is where you can adjust your volume on screen. Most computer keyboard have dedicated volume buttons on them or will use specific F-keys to turn volume up and down. You can also control your volume from the volume icon in the right side of the task bar on the desktop.

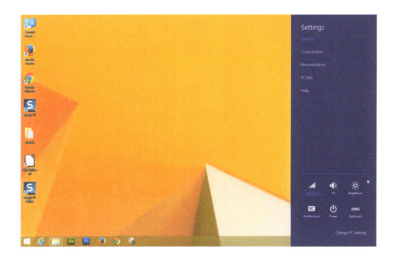

7 PROGRAMS

The Start screen shows you many Microsoft pre-installed or downloaded apps from the Microsoft Store along with creating new Tiles for programs you install manually. The programs or apps from Microsoft or downloaded from the Store are referred to as Modern style apps.

These Modern style apps do have some benefits like "Live Tiles" where you can see up to the minute web based information. They are full screen. This makes them very pretty to look at, but harder to do multi-tasking. I will show you how to resize the windows.

IE takes some getting used to and I prefer and recommend using the desktop version, but that is personal preference. Apps like weather, News, Travel, Finance and even Mail -now that you can copy and paste with 8.1- are very usable

 The News App Full Screen

The Photos app is very slow and cumbersome. I will show you how to make to old Windows Photo Viewer the default photo viewer.

How to Use it...

- **App Store**. Click on the Store tile to be taken to the Microsoft Store to find, buy, and install apps / programs. You will have to sign in with a Microsoft account to download most any app.

* Do Not just ender your password when they tell you to "Switch to a Microsoft account", instead use the "Sign into each app separately instead (not recommended)" link at the bottom of the window that opens.

This refers back chapter 3 and the problems with using a Microsoft account as your user name.

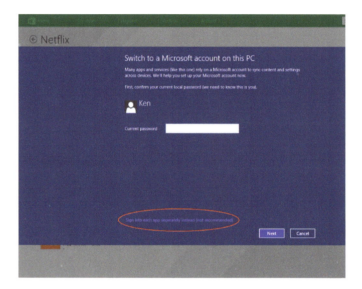

- **Moving to the next screen**. *Use 2 fingers on the mouse pad to move screens sideways or up and down* on Modern style apps and the Start screen.

- **Go to other open windows**. Move the cursor to one of the far left corners of the screen and another Charms like bar –The **App switching bar** - will open showing you the other programs you have open. Click on the one you want to switch to.

- **Multi windows with Modern Apps**.(8.1 only) (this is another long one to explain)
- *Move your cursor to the top of the Modern App > Click and hold > then you can move the window to the side of the screen and release the mouse button.* The program will resize to be half screen. Once that is done, you can open another app from the App Switching bar (see above) or the Taskbar and it will be half screen.

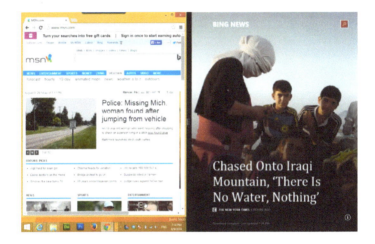

You can resize the windows to have one of them be larger than the other by *grabbing (click and hold) the vertical line in the middle of the 2 apps and drag it left or right.*

- Change default photo program.

Right-click on any photo > *Open with* > *Choose default program* > *Windows Photo Viewer in the window that opens.* Or any other program you may want.

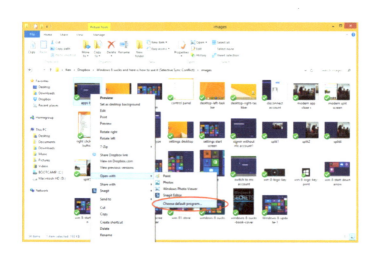

8 THE DESKTOP

Windows 8.0 does not open to the desktop by default; you have to click on the Desktop tile or press the Windows Key on your keyboard. The 8.1 update made the Desktop the default because so many people and business' complained about the Modern Start screen.

Another - and the biggest complaint about Windows 8.0 was that there is no Start menu!

There is still no Start menu in 8.1, but Microsoft added a Start button. The Start button lets you switch between the Desktop and Start screen and some right click options were added like Power.

I underlined menu and button above because they are often used interchangeably and when it was announced that the Start button would come back in the 8.1 Update, everyone thought it was going to be the menu. So when 8.1 Update came out and there was no menu, there were a lot of angry people and web posts.

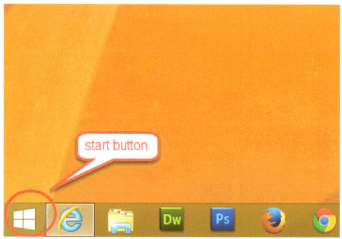

Start button – new in 8.1

How to Use it...

Except for not having the Start menu, the Desktop looks and functions the same as it did in 7. Yay again!

You can right click on the Desktop to "Personalize" your background and screen saver, or start a new folder or text document.

You have the Taskbar at the bottom that has the Start button, pinned programs, notification area, and the time.

Most programs should put an icon on the Desktop – or ask you if you want one.

You can also access the traditional Explorer (My Computer) window.

- **Start button**. Located in the lower left corner, use it to switch between the Desktop and the new Start screen. Right-clicking on it will also bring up Shutdown, Control Panel, and other some useful options you may need some day. Check it out!

- **Taskbar**. Lets you keep a one click link to your most used programs. You can right click it to access its settings and open Task Manager. It will show itself on the Tile screen if you move your cursor to the very bottom of the screen below the slider bar.

- **Notifications area**. Shows you messages from Windows and the programs that are running in the background. You can adjust volume and connect to Internet settings. It also lets you eject your USB device before removing it.

- Add a Start Menu. You can use a 3rd party program to give you a Windows 7 like Start Menu again. I have done this for many of my Windows 8 customers. There are 2 main options here. One is free, the other costs $5 and has a more polished look and couple better features.

- **Classic Shell**. Free (You can donate) and gives you pretty much everything you need. Get it from Classicshell.net

- **Stardock's Start8**. $5 and may be a little more professional looking and has a couple more

features and support. Get it from Stardock.com

9 BLAME IE 11

Windows 8 launched with Internet Explorer (IE) 10. For the most part IE 10 works fine. Some people and business still prefer IE 9, but some web sites are starting to be less reliable on IE 9. In the middle of October 2013 Microsoft released IE 11 to the general user and it was included in Windows Updates.

The Internet stopped working on that day.

No, I'm kidding, but I got a lot of calls starting that week when people could not log on to their bank web site, Netflix, and Yahoo had issues – for quite a while. Even today, the first question I ask if someone says a web site is not working is "Are you using IE 11?" or "Have you tried it in Firefox or Chrome?" Most of the time the site works in one of the other browsers. When I work on a computer I often block IE 11 if it has not already been installed.

Today it mostly works well, but I still notice issues on Netflix and some bank sites.

How to Use it...

If you are not noticing any major issues, I would keep IE 11, but make sure you have another browser like Firefox or Chrome to use if you experience problems. In fact, I suggest using another browser anyway; for security and speed reasons. Both Chrome and Firefox are generally considered safer and less vulnerable to toolbars and home page hijacking.

We are talking about IE on the Desktop. The IE that is part of the Modern / Tile interface can't be removed. (Well, not for this book anyway.)

I will show you how to Restore, Reset, or remove IE 11 to fix basic problems with web pages not working correctly.

- **Restore IE**. Often you can fix minor web issues with the click of a button (Including helping Netflix issues). **Restore Advanced Settings** will restore the programs defaults and fixes many problems people have with IE loading.

With IE open on the Desktop > click on the Settings gear icon in the upper right corner > Internet Options > Advanced Tab on the top right of the window that opens > Restore Advanced Settings button below the list of settings > Apply button at the bottom of the window.
Restart the browser and see how it works.

- **Reset IE**. If Restore did not help, try this. **Reset** will kind of do a quick reinstall IE. It is located in the same window as Restore.

With IE open on the Desktop > click on the settings gear icon in the upper right corner > Internet Options > Advanced Tab on the top right of the window that opens > Reset button below Restore Advanced Settings > Reset in the window that opens for confirmation and options.
Restart the browser and see how that worked.

- **Uninstall IE 11**. *Right-click on the Start menu > Control Panel > Uninstall a program under the Programs heading. Select Turn Windows features on or off located in the left sidebar of the window that opens. Uncheck the Internet Explorer 11 box in the list and click on Ok to complete the process.*

This will take a few minutes, and may need a restart of the computer.

Your computer will revert to having IE 10.

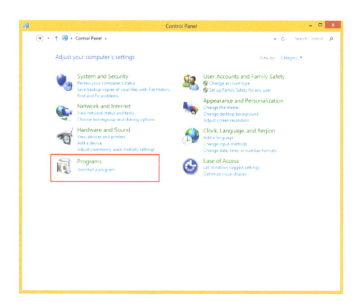

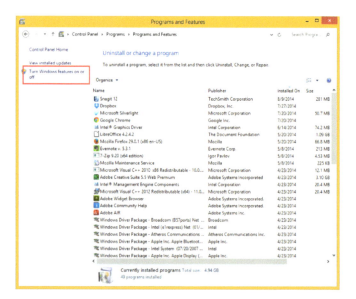

10 THE FUTURE OF 8

This book is being published in the late summer of 2014 and Windows 8 has been around for about 2 years now and is about to get another big update in August, but Microsoft is not calling it Update 2. Just an update. Of course 8 will continue to be developed until 2015 and will get updates until at least 2018.

Windows 8 *will not* be getting a Windows 7 style Start menu!

There were some rumors of 8 getting the 7 style Start menu earlier this year, but Microsoft is keeping it for Windows 9.

Windows 9 code named "Threshold" is set to be released in April of 2015 as of this publication.

There should not be any major changes to 8; everything should be under the hood tweaks and general updates.

There are rumors - RUMORS I say, that Windows 9 may be a free upgrade from8.1. If this is true, I will probably suggest doing that upgrade. 9 should not need any more resources (power) than 8, and since they will be fixing all the problems 8 has it is expected to be a better operating system much like 7 was compared to Vista.

I will be working with the Beta or testing version of 9 as soon as it is available and will have a new book for it. Even though I do not plan on 9 being bad, the book will be titles similar to *Windows 9 Sucks (No it doesn't) and Here's How to Use It.*

ABOUT THE AUTHOR

Ken Barker is a computer technician who has been working on computers for over 10 years. He has worked at Staples and several local computer shops and software companies. He was worked customer support / customer service for most of his life.

Customers always comment on how good Ken is with talking to them and explaining computer / technology stuff in a way they can understand and not be condescending or make them feel stupid.

Ken also runs a technology news site called TechBreakdown.tv where he tries to convey technology news and information in a way that the average person can understand it.

Look for other books from Ken about Android, iOS, OS X, and of course Windows 9 when it come out in 2015.

www.ingramcontent.com/pod-product-compliance
Lightning Source LLC
Chambersburg PA
CBHW041146050326
40689CB00001B/505